D1728297

CONTENTS

Front and back cover photos by San Diego Zoo.

Front endpapers:
A 37-day-old greater sulphur-crested cockatoo baby (largest bird) and baby umbrella cockatoos each approximately 27 days old. Photo by Frank Nothaft.

Back endpapers:
Umbrella cockatoos showing the typical posture of baby cockatoos of their age (slightly less than a month). Photo by Frank Nothaft.

In addition to the photography credits specifically mentioned in accompaniment to individual photos, the following credits apply also: JOHN DANIEL: 23, 38 (1,4); KERRY V. DONNELLY: 16 (top), 20; FRANK NOTHAFT: 6, 8, 9, 10, 11, 16 (bottom), 19, 22, 38-39 (2,3,5) 48, 49, 58, 73, 88 (top), 89; LOUISE VAN DER MEID: 88 (bottom).

t.f.h.

ISBN 0-87666-877-5

Distributed in the U.S. by T.F.H. Publications, Inc., 211 West Sylvania Avenue, PO Box 427, Neptune, NJ 07753; in England by T.F.H. (Gt. Britain) Ltd., 13 Nutley Lane, Reigate, Surrey; in Canada to the book store and library trade by Beaverbooks Ltd., 150 Lesmill Road, Don Mills, Ontario M38 2T5, Canada; in Canada to the pet trade by Rolf C. Hagen Ltd., 3225 Sartelon Street, Montreal 382, Quebec; in Southeast Asia by Y.W. Ong, 9 Loring 36 Geylang, Singapore 14; in Australia and the South Pacific by Pet Imports Pty. Ltd., P.O. Box 149, Brookvale 2100, N.S.W. Australia. Published by T.F.H. Publications, Inc., Ltd., The British Crown Colony of Hong Kong.

BREEDING
COCKATOOS

ANN NOTHAFT

Here the author is shown with one of her sulphur-crested cockatoos; below is a Goffin's cockatoo, another species she has successfully maintained.

photo below by San Diego Zoo.

Introduction

Over the past twelve years, my husband and I have been the owners of many pairs of cockatoos, the species and subspecies being the greater sulphur-crested, bare-eyed, Goffin's, tritons, rose-breasted, lesser sulphur-crested, Timor, Banksian, Eleonora, citron, umbrella and Moluccan. Through the years, most of these birds have been sold off in order to make room for more productive stock. Our collection now consists of greater sulphur-crested cockatoos, Eleonora cockatoos, umbrella cockatoos, Timor cockatoos and lesser sulphur-crested cockatoos. It also contains cockatiels (a mixed variety—albinos, pearlies, pieds and splits), African grey parrots, grand eclectus parrots, Senegal parrots and black-hooded caiques.

1. Like most other parrots, cockatos are very efficient chewers; metal flashing has been installed around an electrical outlet to prevent the birds from chewing through the wiring. 2. A nest log for African grey parrots in the author's aviary. 3. A pair of breeding greater sulphur-crested cockatoos belonging to the author. 4. Ceramic dog bowls, easily cleaned, are used to hold food and water.

3

4

1. Eleonora cockatoo breeders sunning themselves in the outside flight. 2. A pair of Leadbeater's cockatoos shown with their metal garbage can nesting site; note that the can is attached at the highest point in the aviary. Other desirable parrots such as eclectus parrots (3, male; 4, female) and African greys (5) live in harmony with the author's cockatoos by being partitioned off from them within the large indoor aviary. Photos by Frank Nothaft.

1

2

3
4
5

We have always been successful with our cockatiels and have hand-raised many fine babies, much to the delight of their new owners. The next step up was to hand-raise baby cockatoos. This was to us the prime goal in breeding birds. We finally achieved our goal after we purchased a pair of greater sulphur-crested cockatoos *(Cacatua galerita galerita)* from California. The pair has been in our possession for the past eight years. They are absolutely beautiful, and we have raised twelve wonderful babies from this magnificent pair. More babies would have been raised, but we did not have the necessary expertise in the beginning years.

This book is being written in the hope that it will assist the novice breeder in avoiding the pitfalls that we have encountered during the introductory years. By giving a description of our aviaries and equipment and the methods we use to raise our baby birds, we hope to provide general guidelines to serve as steppingstones on the road to avicultural success.

In our opinion, there is no comparison with a hand-raised baby bird. Such a bird is a delight to own because it is completely people-oriented and shows no interest in other birds. Its only concern is for the love and companionship given to it by its owner. Baby birds are very much like young children and should be treated as such, with kindness and understanding. Our baby cockatoos are hand-raised from day one. We cannot begin to tell you the great joy and pride that we derive from successfully hatching, rearing and orienting birds as majestic as the greater sulphur-crested cockatoo. We feel that they are truly the ultimate in pet birds.

Intelligent, curious, affectionate and beautiful, cockatoos are among the most desirable of all pet birds. They will reward their owners with satisfaction in proportion to the amount of affection and good care they receive. Photo by Louise van Der Meid.

Although individual cockatoos vary so greatly in their capacity to imitate the human voice that it is impossible to make hard and fast rules about which species are the best talkers, in general it can be said that the smaller species (such as the red-vented cockatoo, *Cacatua haematopygia,* at left) are less gifted than the mid-size (Leadbeater's or Major Mitchell cockatoo, *Cacatua leadbeateri,* shown below) and large species. Photos by San Diego Zoo.

Talking Ability

This book is specifically about breeding cockatoos, and teaching a cockatoo to talk therefore is not properly an important part of it, but I'd like to make a few general remarks about cockatoos' talking ability in general.

Much has been written about the African grey parrot and several species of Amazon parrots as gifted talkers. Cockatoos, on the other hand, have been labeled as "indifferent" talkers. It is my opinion, based on my personal observation of many species of cockatoos, that this labeling is quite untrue. No two birds of the same species, whether they are cockatoos or any other parrots, will have the same talking ability. The fact is that cockatoos and other parrots

Cockatoos are natural performers whether they're showing off for their owners or among other birds—and of course the possession of a large crest helps a bird to attract attention to itself.

have such variable individual personalities that you can't generalize about species—you can only remark about talking ability on a bird-by-bird basis.

An extremely tame, affectionate and intelligent bird means more to me than its ability to talk. Cockatoos are such intelligent birds that if they are given the attention they need they will not only speak well but also will do tricks with ease. It is really up to the owner of the bird as to just how much the bird will say or do. The bird has the capacity for speech, but you have to bring it out.

The greater sulphur-crested cockatoo has a clearly audible voice and becomes an extremely gifted talker. In general, as the cockatoo's size decreases, so does the volume of its voice.

A hand-fed baby cockatoo has such an affectionate disposition and enjoys its owner's presence so much that it is not hard to have the bird say at least a few simple phrases. The owner of the cockatoo determines just how many words the bird will say by the amount of time he puts into the bird.

Young cockatoos learn to talk at various ages. I have had several baby cockatoos speak at three months of age. One of these birds, a greater sulphur-crested, said "Hello," "Hello, Lenny," "Atta boy" and "Come here." A three-year-old greater sulphur-crested youngster named "Moose" has a wide variety of sentences, some of them more than five words long. This bird learned a few words during his first year, building up his vocabulary during his second year; now in his third year, he's still learning new words. This bird also sings and dances when asked to. "Moose" is an intelligent and delightfully affectionate pet.

Teaching a cockatoo to talk is the same as teaching any other type of parrot. First, pick a simple two-word phrase. Repeat this phrase over and over, always using the same level of pitch and tone to your voice. The first time the cockatoo repeats a new word or phrase, it may not be very clear. As the bird repeats it, the words become clearer. It is

17

1. and 2. Talented cockatoos performing tricks at Paradise Park, Hawaii. 3. Regardless of what you want to teach your bird to do, whether it's to talk or perform in some other manner, always remember that it responds to affection and gentle care.

1

2

very much like a young child learning to speak. As the bird learns a new word or phrase, move on to another.

Repetition is the key to teaching any cockatoo or parrot to talk. This can become very monotonous, which is one of the reasons people give up so easily when trying to teach a bird to talk. The use of a tape recorder can be incorporated into the teaching-to-talk sessions. By making a tape loop of the phrase you want the bird to learn, you can play it when you are out of the house. You can then repeat the phrase to the bird when the tape is not being used. The teaching method is entirely up to the individual owner of the bird.

3

The once-sturdy two-by-four on which this bird is perched has been worked over; any wood framing in a cockatoo's living quarters must be either protected by sheathing or replaced periodically. Below: a cockatoo in flight in the author's aviary. Comparatively large birds like cockatoos must be provided with sufficient room to exercise.

Our Aviary

It is difficult to describe the aviary in which we raise our cockatoos without giving you a brief history of the building as it was prior to being converted into an aviary. This explanation will help make the visualizing of the aviary simpler. Also, it will give you a clearer understanding of how you can improvise buildings (garages, coops, sheds).

The building that is now our aviary was originally built in 1931 as a chicken coop for a commercial poultry farm. In 1963, our neighbor, the owner of the poultry business, made us an offer to acquire one of his coops, as he had given up the business a few years prior. At this particular time my husband and I had an interest only in such birds as

1. A sulphur-crested cockatoo perched on its feeding platform; the branch leading from the platform gives the bird easy access. 2. The author administering a vitamin-mineral supplement and (3) sharing a contemplative moment with one of her prized pets.

1

2

chickens, pigeons and geese. We purchased the coop with the intention of consolidating all of our stock under one roof. We engaged house movers and had the building moved to our property. A six-inch poured concrete floor was put in immediately, followed by the remodeling of the coop. The building was divided to accommodate pigeons and chickens in one half, and the other half was used for utilities and storage.

In 1964 we purchased our first parrot and by 1965 we had decided to explore the breeding of exotic birds. At this point, the decision was made to move the chickens and pigeons to other lodgings and convert the building into an aviary.

CONSTRUCTION OF THE AVIARY

Basically, our aviary is an insulated building that is 24 feet wide by 42 feet long, without the outdoor screen flights added. The front of the building faces south. The main door is on the west side. On the north side, a large door (4 feet wide by 7 feet high) allows entry to the feed and storage room. This door is hinged so that it can be opened halfway to enter or all the way to accommodate large items being stored or taken out.

As you enter the building from the west door, a 42-foot-long aisle runs down the middle of the aviary. Seven flights line the right-hand side of the aisle. On the left side, the sink, feed mixing table and oil hot air heater are encountered. Four more flights, the feed storage room and one more large flight that has a portable partition (so that it may be made into two flights if necessary) make up the left side of the aisle.

The building is a basic wooden frame structure. It consists of 2 x 4″ studs, tongue and groove sheathing and asbestos shingles. The roof is 10 feet high at the peak, pitching down to 7 feet on both sides, with a 2-foot overhang.

The original building, the chicken coop, had windows

running completely across the entire length of the south side, which is 42 feet long. The original windows were wooden storm windows. We knew that they could not possibly stand up to cockatoos and other parrots, so we changed them to aluminum sliding windows. These seemed perfect because the glass panels were designed to be removed in their entirety with ease. This comes in handy, because we remove them for the hot summer months. At this time they are cleaned and stored away until October. In the fall we replace them, gradually closing them as the weather gets chilly. The windows remain closed permanently for the winter, thus forcing the birds to remain indoors, and are opened a little at a time in the spring.

In the beginning we had left the passageway open so that the birds had access to the outdoor flights. We observed, though, that during our severe winter months the birds rarely entered the outdoor flights. We also had the problem that the water for the birds froze, thus breaking the water dishes and depriving the birds of water. This problem was resolved by closing the birds in for most of the winter (December 15th - February 15th) and keeping the aviary temperature at 42°F. The heat is maintained by a fuel oil furnace.

We feel that the birds actually do not gain anything by being wintered outdoors in this climate, as it can do more harm than good. Many successful bird breeders do fine with their birds being confined indoors all year long. At the same time, however, many bird breeders have had good results by keeping their birds wintered out of doors, with nothing more than thin plastic (polyethylene) covering their flights.

If the winters are severe in your area and you choose to allow your birds access to the out of doors during this winter weather, you *must* supply them with an appropriate shelter. This shelter should be weatherproofed to provide high and dry perches and feed.

The greater sulphur-crested cockatoo, *Cacatua galerita galerita*, is native to Australia and grows to a length of about 20 inches. Photo by San Diego Zoo.

The lesser sulphur-crested cockatoo, *Cacatua sulphurea sulphurea*, is considerably smaller (growing to only about 13 inches) than the greater sulphur-crested and has a more northerly distribution, mainly on the island of Celebes. Photo by Paradise Park, Hawaii.

A case in point is that of an owner who kept his double yellow head parrot in a large outdoor aviary during the winter without adequate shelter. When freezing rains came, the bird had no shelter to protect it from the severe weather conditions. Consequently, the freezing rain froze the parrot's feet to the perch. The parrot, in order to free itself, bit its feet off. As you can see, this tragedy would have been avoided had the owner used common sense.

In our Long Island area, hawks are also a winter problem. Occasionally large numbers pass over our aviary during their migratory flight. The fact that their food supply is limited at this time often causes these birds to throw caution to the wind—their hunger apparently brings out the boldness in these predators. We have often observed these birds in trees surrounding our aviary. Occasionally one has been seen actually sitting atop one of the flights. On one rare occasion a sparrow hawk actually swooped down in pursuit of a colony of cockatiels in an outdoor flight. Apparently it was so desperate that it saw only the birds and not the wire surrounding them. This hawk actually flew full force, slammed into the wire and then fell to the ground in a momentary state of unconsciousness. Within minutes it appeared to come to its senses and flew away. However, this incident caused our birds two broken wings, a broken neck and a bloody beak, plus complete havoc through the aviary. Following this, the birds were uneasy for three or four days. Again, this situation was eliminated by keeping the birds indoors during the winter.

When birds have to be caught up for one reason or another, the small passageway becomes convenient. Birds are encouraged to enter the inside flight through the hole and the passage is closed off with ease, making the capture of the birds an effortless task.

All other windows in the building are double hung wooden windows. Removable wire panels cover these windows, making access for opening, closing and cleaning simple. There is at least one good-size window in every flight. The passageways in these flights are appropriate size holes that were cut through the walls just to the side of the window. These holes were then edged with metal to deter destructive chewing. Small metal covers were made for these holes to open and close them whenever necessary.

The building is completely insulated with four-inch-fiberglass insulation. Masonite wallboard was applied over this as a final covering. All seams and edges were covered with metal stripping, and again this was done in order to discourage destruction. We have found that this works well, because Masonite has an extremely smooth surface. With all edges and seams secured, the birds cannot get a start in chewing. All other wooden construction in the flights is covered with metal or heavy gauge wire mesh. Chewing is good exercise and entertainment for cockatoos and other parrots. This fondness for chewing is quite annoying to the aviculturist, who must keep a constant vigil over the aviaries, making sure that the birds do not escape. Thick pieces of scrap wood such as 2 x 4's, 4 x 6's, etc., are hung in the flights for the birds' chewing enjoyment. Care is always taken in the choice of this wood, making certain that it is not contaminated by paint or a wood treatment that could possibly cause illness. The wood is usually replaced frequently, as the birds quickly reduce it to a pile of splinters. All electrical wires are run through conduit tubing, and all lights are covered with heavy wire mesh.

OUTDOOR FLIGHTS

The outdoor flights for the cockatoos and larger parrots are made of heavy 11 gauge wire, similar to chainlink fencing. The dimensions of one of these flights is 4 feet high, 4 feet wide and 15 feet long. This wire is used on all sides and also on the top and bottom. This flight is three feet off the ground. There are three more flights made of the same material. The dimensions of these are 4 feet high, 5 feet

1. Salmon-crested cockatoo, *Cacatua moluccensis,* from the Moluccas Islands. 2. Goffin's cockatoo, *Cacatua goffini,* from the Tanimbar Islands. 3. Rose-breasted cockatoo, also called galah, *Eolophus roseicapillus;* this bird ranges over a wide area of Australia. Photos: 1, Vogelpark Walsrode; 2. A. J. Mobbs; 3. Dr. Herbert R. Axelrod.

1

2

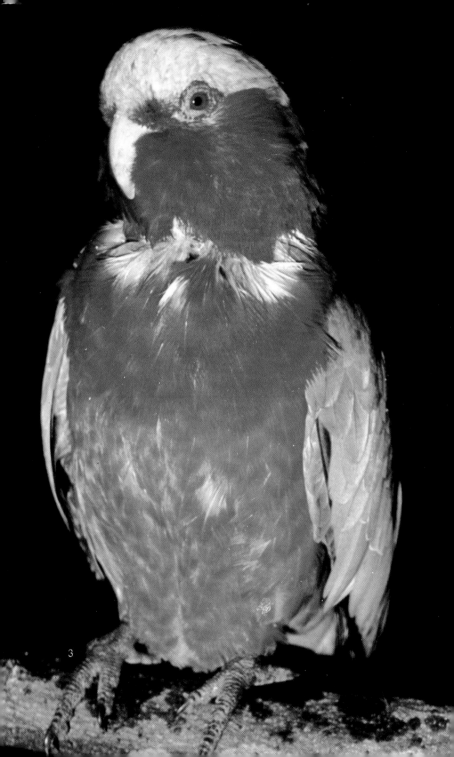

long and 4 feet wide. These are 18 inches off the ground. (Our breeding pair of greater sulphur-crested cockatoos has one of these outdoor flights.) The reason for having these four flights off the ground was to best utilize the material we had on hand and to make for very effective ease of maintenance. They are also completely covered in one-inch mesh to prevent the entering of sparrows. Raising the flights off the ground seems to have been very effective against mice and other vermin, as we have no problem with either of these creatures.

Flights for our cockatiels and smaller parrots are made of 1x2" welded wire with a 2x4" wood framing. Framing should be on the outside to prevent chewing. If any of the wood framing is on the inside, it is covered with sheet metal.

We have two kinds of partitions in the outdoor flight. The first kind of partition is in the flights of the cockatoos. They are of corrugated metal in order to stop visual distraction from birds of the same species. An example of this is a pair of lesser sulphur-cresteds, which are housed next door to a pair of greater sulphur-cresteds. Before this metal separation was put into place, the pairs were always lunging at each other or hanging onto the wire trying to fight with each other.

The partitions are of double wire, with a 4-inch space between them. This is used to prevent physical contact which would cause injury to the neighboring birds. We find some pairs of two different species are very compatible being next door to each other in adjoining flights. An example of such birds is a pair of African greys whose outside flight is next to that of a pair of Eleonora cockatoos. They have double wire partitions between them. These birds are very consistent, showing no interest in or fear of each other.

The 2-foot overhang on the building provides partial shade in all of the flights. In the longer flights we also have 4 feet of the roof covered on the opposite end with corrugated fiberglass patio roofing.

We have found that on hot summer days the birds go outside only during early morning and late afternoon. This excludes rainy days, as all of our bird really enjoy bathing in the rain. It has also been observed that just before dark all of our birds enter the inside flights and quietly roost for the night. They have *never* been observed attempting to sleep in the outside flights during the night. They come inside of their own accord, and they have never had to be coaxed inside.

All perches are branches cut from tree limbs. They are placed at the farthest distance from each other and at different heights to encourage flying for exercise. These branches are chosen in different thicknesses to accommodate birds of different sizes. The thicker branches are for larger birds and the thinner ones for the smaller birds. If branches are too large or too small to accommodate the birds' feet, they will not be comfortable for roosting. This could also make "treading" (mating) more complicated. Be sure all branches are tightly secured, because wobbly or swaying perches would cause the same conditions.

We leave all of the bark on the branches but cut off all small twiglike branches. In this way, the birds cannot possibly injure their wings when flying. If these small branches were not removed, they would be chewed off within an hour or so anyway, so we feel that it is foolish to take a chance for such a short period of time. We supply scrap wood and branches specifically for chewing purposes.

INDOOR FLIGHTS

The sizes of the indoor flights vary slightly. The dimensions of the flight that houses our breeding pair of greater sulphur-crested cockatoos is 6 feet wide by 8 feet long. It has a pitched roof, so the height is 7 feet in front running to 9 feet in the back.

The nest box is hung in the corner of the 9-foot-high section and is out of sight to all other birds and humans. In flights that have multiple nest boxes the boxes are hung in various places in the flights, but all are hung up as high as possible. Through trial and observation, we have found that all boxes hung at low levels were completely disregarded by the birds. They never even bothered to investigate them. In every instance the high boxes were preferred.

All perches hung in these flights are strategically arranged. Care is taken with this arrangement so that no droppings fall into the seed and water dishes. One branch always leads to the hole in the nest box, another is always placed in front of the exit passage to the outside flights, and one is placed in front of the feeding station. All branches are the same type used in the outdoor flights.

The flight partitions consist of plywood covered over with wire. This was done to give individual pairs complete privacy in the breeding area of their flight.

All the walls inside the flights are painted either dark brown or black or are natural wood. When the aviary was first constructed most indoor flights were painted white. This was done to create a brighter atmosphere for the birds. We soon realized that the birds did not look content in their bright surroundings and were showing no signs of breeding. The flights that were not painted were of dark natural wood. Birds housed in these were more active and were working their nest boxes. We then painted the white flights dark, which gave the interior moderate light. Once this was done the birds had their sense of privacy and seclusion restored, and then breeding commenced. When painting any material that birds will have access to, be certain to use only paint which states "non-toxic" on the label.

All aviaries are accessible through individual doors lining the main aisle. All flights have a large screened-in portion facing the main aisle. In all cases this incorporates the feeding stations. This screened portion is great for observing the birds and at the same time not disturbing their privacy.

As you can see by the dimensions of the above flights,

they are not at all huge. However, we do feel that they provide adequately for our birds. It has been mentioned many times in other texts that enormous flights are required for cockatoos and other large parrots, the reason being that the birds require the flying space provided by these flights in order to remain physically fit and to prevent possible egg binding. The aforementioned is all quite true, but we believe that climbing is also good. When observing a bird climbing, you can clearly see all the different muscles that are being put to use. Climbing appears to utilize all muscle groups in the body, from head to tail. Only on occasion are the wings used for leverage in the climbing process. We feel that a bird that is an active climber is keeping its body physically fit. It would not seem to matter to muscles around the reproductive system of the bird whether the wing muscles are not as strong as they would be in the wild or in an enormous aviary. There are reported successful breedings from both cock and hen birds (large hookbills) with one or both wings pinioned. Bearing in mind that a pinioned bird can never fly, it would seem to substantiate our opinions. This is not to say that we would not love to have enormous flights which would afford both climbing and flying pleasures to the birds—it's just that it is possible to breed the birds without having such quarters.

Through the years we have had eggs from the following birds without any problems of egg binding: Eleonoras, tritons, greater sulphurs, Moluccans, bare-eyeds, citrons and rose-breasted cockatoos, as well as grand eclectus and Senegal parrots.

FEEDING STATIONS

Feeding is made simple by the use of feeding stations. These are fully accessible through a small hinged door incorporated into the screened portion of the flights. Just inside the door is a wire platform measuring 18 x 24 inches. To stop the dishes from falling off, the platform is equipped with a 1-inch rim around the edge. This station is large enough to hold all feeding dishes. These are braced securely underneath by metal shelf brackets. As I have stated before, each of these platforms has a perch leading to it for the birds' convenience when feeding.

SIZE AND KINDS OF NEST BOXES

Before a pair of cockatoos is introduced to a flight, two nest boxes of appropriate size are installed. One is always a metal garbage can, and the other is most often a wooden box. Providing two boxes enables the birds to make a choice. Most often they choose the metal type, in which case we remove the wooden one, replacing it with another metal one. This then allows the birds a choice of nesting sites.

The sizes of the boxes and entrance holes in them vary according to the size of the birds. The large cockatoos get 20-gallon garbage cans with a 7-inch diameter round entrance hole. The smaller cockatoos and parrots get 12-gallon garbage cans with a 5-inch entrance hole. The entrance holes should be just large enough so that the birds can go through with ease. Wooden boxes differ in shape, but all are about the same size. All wooden boxes should be covered both inside and outside with wire to prevent destructive chewing. A small door is made in the side for care and observation.

All metal nest boxes have the bottom bent into a concave shape to prevent the eggs from rolling. The entrance hole is placed 3 inches from the top of the can. To make the interior of the nest box climbable, a strip of wire netting is fastened to the side from just below the entrance hole down to the bottom on the inside of the box. The wire should stand away from the wall of the box in order to act as a ladder. This must be done so that the birds may climb in and out easily. If this wire were not supplied, birds could still use the nest box, but they would enter it clumsily and cause possible damage to eggs or young chicks.

The boxes are hung on the wall as high as possible and are fastened in a way so that they may be taken down easily. Care is always taken to be certain that they are secure and will not wobble or shift when being used by the birds. Cockatoos nest in the hollows of trees in the wild, usually near water. The bottoms of these nests contain damp decayed wood which the birds rearrange to their liking.

To simulate this, the nesting material used in all boxes is a mixture of 50% shredded sugar cane, 25% peat moss and 25% pine shavings. The shredded sugar cane is obtained at a feed supply store under the name of "Sta-Dry" and comes in a bale containing approximately 6 cubic feet. Approximately 6 inches of this material is put in each box.

CLEANING OF FLIGHTS AND AVIARY

Once weekly the aisles are swept and the droppings cleaned out of each flight. Birds are creatures of habit and roost on the same perch, making the picking up of their droppings quite easy. The shavings placed on the floor of each flight absorb the droppings; they can be scooped up quickly in a metal dust pan. Apart from a few seeds and feathers on the floor, the shavings stay remarkably clean. Dustless pine shavings are the kind used.

The entire aviary is thoroughly cleaned twice a year, once just before breeding season begins (around the end of February) and once again after breeding season is over (the beginning of October). Each flight has the food, water, grit, mineral and salt blocks removed. The shavings on the floor are picked up and the flights are vacuumed to remove all dust and webs that have accumulated. Cockatoos give off excessive amounts of powder (especially when in good health), which accounts for all the dust. The aisles and feed storage room are also vacuumed. All walls are washed down with a strong germicidal disinfectant, and all flights and

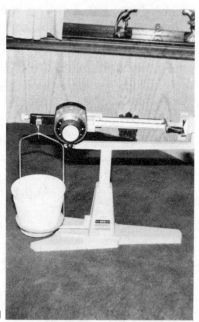

perches are sprayed with a mild mite spray. This has kept our birds free of mites. After all of the steps listed above have been taken, clean shavings are then placed on the floors. We have found that a good workshop-type vacuum cleaner does a very good job and makes the task of cleaning much easier.

The shavings on the floor harbor and breed mealworms. All of our birds scratch in the shavings in search of these mealworms and promptly eat them. I do not know how the birds are aware that they are there, but it is a good source of protein for them.

We find that the less the birds are disturbed, the better the pairs like it. That is why major cleaning is done only twice a year, with quick weekly cleanings, so as to disturb them as little as possible. They really do enjoy their privacy.

1. Note how the joints in the hardboard, visible behind the birds, have been covered with metal strips to eliminate chewing. 2. Scale used by the author to keep accurate track of the weight of developing baby birds. 3. Partial view of the food storage area in the author's aviary. 4. A view down the center aisle of the aviary. 5. Food preparation area in the aviary.

5

Besides being able to use their feet to bring food to their mouths, cockatoos also use them to grasp a wide range of objects. Photo by Kerry V. Donnelly. Below: bare-eyed cockatoos (also known as little corellas), *Cacatua sanguinea*, at their water dish. Cockatoos **must** be provided with clean fresh water at all times. Photo by L. Moon.

Feeding

The food and water dishes used for the cockatoos are large 8-inch ceramic dog bowls. The smaller birds get ceramic bowls appropriate to their size. The bowls are heavy in weight so the bird cannot tip them and thereby spill the contents. Another nice feature is the fact that they are very easy to wash and keep clean.

The food and water dishes are washed daily with dishwashing detergent and water. Once a week they are washed with a good strong disinfectant. I cannot stress too strongly the washing of the dishes. The water dishes can get a germ-producing slime in just one day, so it is best to play it safe and wash them with care. Some birds dump their seeds in the water dishes, which swiftly fouls the water.

It is strange, but some birds are very neat with their eating habits and others are extremely sloppy. Our pair of grand eclectus falls into the sloppy category. Their water must be changed twice a day, especially during the hot summer months, because they throw so much seed into it.

All pairs have a large bowl of mineralized grit available at all times. Some pairs pick at the grit and others just ignore it entirely. I really cannot explain this, but when you own and observe birds for long periods of time, they will all show that they are individuals, exhibiting different habits. You soon will see that no two are alike, even in the same species.

Mineralized salt blocks and mineral blocks hang in each flight. The salt blocks are bought in a feed supply store, but the mineralized blocks are made up by us. The mineral block recipe consists of the following:

3 parts plaster

5 parts powdered limestone

2 or 3 parts bone meal

1 part mineralized gravel

The above ingredients are mixed with water to make a soup-like consistency and then poured into large paper cups which serve as molds. As this mixture dries, a U-shaped wire is inserted in the top. This wire is used to hang the block up. Allow this mixture to cure in the paper cups one week. Then peel off the paper cup and you have a nice mineral block to hang in your flights. You can of course purchase ready-made mineral blocks at your petshop if you don't want to go to all the trouble of making your own.

All our newly purchased birds are quarantined for 60 days. By "quarantined" I mean that they are kept apart from our established stock. They are fed boiled water along with the regular diet. The reason for giving them boiled water is that water is different in all parts of the country. Birds, just like people, get diarrhea from drinking water they are not accustomed to. I boil up two quarts of water at a time (boiling for 10 minutes) and then refrigerate. This boiled water is then given to the birds for two weeks. At the end of two weeks, the mixture consists of half boiled water and half regular tap water. This is given one week. The fourth week the water consists of ¾ tap water and ¼ boiled water. Straight regular tap water is introduced at the end of the fourth week.

An important aspect to consider when buying birds is to ask what they are being fed. Birds are creatures of habit and may not eat when suddenly introduced to a new feed mix. It is best to give the birds what they were used to and introduce new items to their diet as the birds acclimate themselves to your aviaries. If for some reason you cannot acquire the birds' previous diet, you must offer them quite a variety of food until you happen on a food to their liking. Feed this food and introduce new food daily. Cockatoos and other parrots will eat just about any food you desire them to have if you present that food to them often enough.

The nutrition of a cockatoo is a very important topic. Birds will not remain in good health and condition on plain seed alone. A varied diet will provide you with the enjoyment of a healthier and prettier bird. All birds need carbohydrates, fats, proteins, vitamins and minerals to maintain a healthy body and glossy plumage. Through trial and error we have found a diet that is working well with our birds, as they are all healthy and sleek of plumage.

The birds are fed daily on a food mix consisting of:
3 parts sunflower seed
1 part safflower seed
1 part pine nuts (pinon nuts)
1 part canary and parakeet mix
1 part high protein dog meal or monkey chow.
I alternate the dog meal and monkey chow and add a few raw peanuts in the shell for each pair. Once a week I add one part rabbit pellets to this mix.

A ready-made powdered vitamin and mineral supplement

is also added to the above mix. This powder coats the seeds; as the bird moves the seed around in its mouth to crack it, it is sure to consume the vitamins off the seed.

You must remember that climate and availability of seeds are different in all parts of the country and the world, so you have to adapt to what is available. If certain seeds are not available, you are forced to substitute ones that are.

A slice of whole wheat bread is given to each pair twice a week. Plenty of greens are fed daily. I have found that our birds enjoy vegetables more than fruit. Your birds may be the opposite, as all birds are individuals. The two main greens that I feed are spinach and dandelions. The dandelions are the large ones that you purchase in a supermarket or farm stand. These two greens contain calcium, iron, vitamin A and vitamin C. All our birds enjoy eating them. I also supplement with carrots, carrot tops, stringbeans, peas, apples and grapes. All greens, vegetables and fruit should be washed well before feeding, as this insures the removal of all insecticides.

A liquid B-12 supplement is a good appetite stimulant and promotes feather growth. It worked very well on a bird (black hooded caique) that was in poor feather. A few drops were added to the water daily; within two months a noticeable improvement in the bird's feathering had been noted.

Twenty-gallon garbage cans lined with plastic trash bags make very good seed containers. One can for each different kind of seed is used. Plastic bleach bottles, washed and cut out to form a scoop, are placed in each storage container.

When feeding, you should try to wear the same type and color clothing. Any sharp change in color or clothing habits (wearing a hat, for example, when you normally do not) causes extreme tenseness and excitement on the birds' part.

Our neighbor the poultry farmer told us this even before we owned exotic birds. He said that when he changed his way of dress his hens would get frightened and stop laying. The biggest problem with fright was the fleeing of the hens to one corner, piling on top of each other, resulting in the bottom birds' smothering to death. Our exotic birds reacted to a drastic change of dress by becoming very nervous and fidgety. Some let forth with loud screams. Birds have keen vision and can distinguish colors, which would account at least in part for this reaction.

FEEDING FOR BREEDING

The basic feed mix is used when feeding just prior to and during breeding season, the only difference being that rabbit pellets are fed daily instead of once a week. They are fed for their alfalfa content.

The vitamins are the same (a powdered vitamin and mineral supplement on the food) except that a vitamin with electrolytes is added to the water once a week. This is a highly concentrated vitamin for the drinking water. It is an appetite stimulant and helps during periods of stress or disease.

Greens, vegetables, fruit and whole wheat bread are fed in greater quantities, with a sprinkling of wheat germ oil on them. Cod liver oil and egg food are not fed, as they go rancid too rapidly.

When feeding your birds, just remember to use common sense and pick the seed, greens, fruits and vegetables with the highest nutritional value. If you are going to feed egg food or use cod liver oil, remember how fast these foods spoil and remove the uneaten portion the same day.

Patience is one of the keynotes in the breeding of cockatoos, but the birds often give clues to their willingness to breed. Examination of the nesting site by the potential breeders, as shown at left, is a good sign. Below: a male greater sulphur-crested owned by the author engaging in a pre-breeding display for his mate.

Signs of Breeding

Before you attempt to breed cockatoos for the first time, you should realize that it is an endeavor for the truly patient hobbyist and not for someone intent on monetary gain. Patience is the key word, as it takes years to find a steady pair of birds that will successfully reproduce.

Many times we have put a cock and hen together and have been glad to note that their actions looked encouraging. With the passing years, their actions looked more and more promising. Before we knew it, five or six years had elapsed.

We have been through all of the following situations with various pairs of birds:

1. Mating was observed, but no eggs were produced.
2. Eggs were produced but were infertile, and no mating was observed.
3. Mating was observed and eggs were produced, but the eggs were infertile.
4. Mating was observed and fertile eggs were produced. The eggs, however, did not hatch; the embryos grew only so far and then stopped.
5. Mating was observed and fertile eggs produced and hatched. The chicks were found dead or were eaten by the parents.
6. Mating was observed and eggs laid, but the parents ate the eggs.
7. Mating was observed and fertile eggs produced, and the parent birds hatched the eggs. The young were taken and fed by hand or left with the parent birds with the hope that they would do a good job in raising the young.

Quite a number of times, we had birds go through the first six stages mentioned above, never successfully rearing any young from these pairs. Because of this, we frequently lost faith in the pairs. They were then either traded or sold to other breeders. Some of these breeders reported success with the pairs, but others had none. Who is to say whether we would have had the same results had we kept them?

This is by no means meant as a discouragement to novice breeders. I only mean to stress the key word for this hobby, which is PATIENCE. Bird breeding is a great challenge and highly rewarding when a truly enthusiastic aviculturist finally accomplishes his goal.

MATING DANCE

The middle of every February finds our greater sulphur-crested cockatoos starting their mating ritual. The male struts along the perch and displays for the female. His crest is raised, his wings are opened and his tail is fanned out. He utters chattering sounds while he bobs his head up and down, at the same time swaying it side to side in what appears to be a motion resembling a figure eight. After this, they preen each other and touch beaks. They practice this courting ritual quite a number of times before the actual mating takes place.

When they are ready to mate, the hen crouches down on the perch, with her head forward. The cock grabs her by the back of the neck with his beak in what appears to be a sure grip; then he steps slowly onto her back. He centers himself on her back, gripping securely with his feet, putting his tail down to the side of the hen's and wrapping it under hers. While he does this, she lifts her tail slightly to help accommodate this motion. By that time the cock's wings are spread and flapping in order to help keep his balance, as he has to go way off balance to wrap his tail under the hen's in order to mate. They are seen doing this a number of times daily until the eggs are laid.

The hen is frequently observed entering the nest box daily. She proceeds to take out all the nesting material, leaving a little on the sides, with the center dug down to the bottom of the box.

We know the first day that the hen starts working the box because each fall it is filled with fresh nesting material. None is thrown out on the floor until breeding season begins. This particular pair never enters the nest box unless they are working it to lay eggs. We have another pair that we call "box dwellers." As soon as you enter the aviary, they dive into the box and do not come out until they hear us leaving. We rarely see this pair, but we know all is well by the amount of food consumed and an occasional look into the nest box.

This pair of greater sulphur-crested cockatoos always has their first clutch of eggs (two eggs to a clutch) around the tenth of March. Incubation lasts thirty days, and both the cock and hen brood (sit on the eggs). The cock sits during the day and the hen sits at night.

MISCELLANEOUS REMARKS
ABOUT BREEDING

It is a good idea to use night lights in your aviary. We have two 25-watt night lights. They are situated in the aisle, one on each end. This allows a small amount of light to shine into each flight. The lights should be kept on at night throughout the whole year. In the event that the birds are startled off their perches or off the nest, enough light is provided to allow them to find their way back.

Cockatoos that are in good condition and kept in outdoor flights can be heard at least a mile away and farther than that with the wind from them to you. Bear this in mind when you are thinking of housing them outdoors. Your neighbors may not take too kindly to this extremely loud screaming. The screaming usually starts at daybreak and is not favorable to late sleepers.

When cockatoos are in outdoor flights, care must be taken to be sure all construction is sufficiently secure. This precaution is necessary because cockatoos have great power in their beaks. The destruction one of these birds can cause is not to be believed until you own them. Once they escape they are very rarely seen again, because they are good fliers and cover distances quickly.

Because the birds have individual preferences for particular surroundings, they may not like what you give them at first, and it may be necessary to switch them to another flight. This must be done if a pair does not look especially content and appears never really to be settling down. The signs of this are that the birds always seem tense and are never observed to show any interest in the nest boxes. Often when such birds are relocated they settle down and show signs of breeding. We always try to allow sufficient time to elapse in order for the birds to adapt to their new surroundings. Our judgement of time varies according to how wild the birds are when they are first introduced to their flights.

Our breeding pair of greaters had to have their flight changed. They occupied one flight for a little over a year but never looked content, so they were moved to a new flight and had fertile eggs the same year.

In order to have success in breeding, it is very important to be methodical in the care and treatment of your birds. They must feel safe and secure before they will breed, so privacy and seclusion are musts.

During breeding season, our aviaries are off limits to all visitors. Even my husband, who does all of the maintaining and building, is not allowed to enter the aviaries. The birds associate him with the noise that goes along with these chores. When he enters, the birds act uneasy and even get off their eggs until he leaves. I have no problem with this, as I do all the feeding and the birds have complete confidence in me.

Keeping a complete record book on all your birds' activities will prove to be a valuable aid in breeding. In the book that I keep, I write down all the birds' activities including changes in diet, breeding records and data on each baby that I raise. I also write down anything of interest that I hear or read about pertaining to birds and their care and maintenance. My record book is literally a goldmine of information. This book consists of a looseleaf binder that has index tabs indicating the various sections of the book. This makes finding the information that is required very convenient.

The egg of a pair of um-
brella cockatoos, *Cacatua
alba;* the parent birds step-
ped on the egg and made a
large hole in it while the
chick was pipping its way
out. Below: a one-day-old
umbrella cockatoo chick.
Photos by Frank Nothaft.

Incubation

Our greater sulphur-crested cockatoos lay two white eggs per clutch. The second egg is laid the day after the day following the laying of the first egg. Under normal conditions, the eggs take thirty days to hatch. The first egg hatches two days before the second egg.

During incubation, both hen and cock have been observed leaving the nest to feed and returning promptly. This was practiced only during the first two weeks. After this, each bird sat tight, leaving the nest only when being relieved by its mate.

Starting the week before the eggs are due to hatch, the water bowl is found empty every day. During the day, the

cock comes off the nest and the hen replaces him. He splashes around in the water, eats a little and goes back to nest; when he returns, the hen leaves. Sometimes the hen does this bathing just before she goes to the nest to relieve the cock for the night. This is apparently done to provide adequate moisture for the eggs to hatch.

According to my record book, this particular pair has been going to nest for the past five years on or about March 10. This pair also has had a second clutch four out of the past five years. Each clutch had different circumstances surrounding its laying and brooding. In all cases the birds had their second clutch ten to twenty days after the eggs or chicks were removed from the first clutch.

REASONS FOR REMOVING EGGS
OR YOUNG FROM PARENTS

Previous to the past five years, two clutches of eggs were taken from the parents and put in an incubator. We had purchased the best incubator we could find at the time. The first clutch did not get enough humidity, so the chicks stuck to the shell and died. The second clutch was also placed in the incubator, but with the humidity raised. This time the humidity was too high, causing the chicks to drown in the high liquid content of the egg. My husband and I were heartbroken. We had taken the eggs from the parents because they kept getting off the nest. After having done our very best and still not succeeding, we decided to let the parents incubate the following season and hatch the eggs themselves.

In March, 1974 two eggs were laid. The parents incubated the full thirty days. After the thirty days, we noticed that the birds had stopped sitting. The eggs were checked and found to be cold. They were then opened and found to be fertile, but development of the chicks had stopped in the early stages, apparently as the result of a chill.

Two more eggs were laid in the latter part of April. The

birds sat very tight. We contained our curiosity by not going near the nest. We knew the eggs were due to hatch by the end of May. The birds continued to sit tight into June. No observation on our part was made until chicks were heard loudly peeping in the box. Because of the intensity of their cry, we inspected the box and discovered two chicks about one week of age. Their tiny crops were empty, so we decided to take the chicks and feed them by hand. Ten weeks later, we had two beautiful full-grown youngsters.

Early in March, 1975 one of the pair was constantly in the nest. We assumed they had eggs. Between March 14 and 16, however, the birds were neglecting the nest box. On March 17, we checked the nest and found two fertile eggs, but they were ice cold.

At the end of March, the pair went to nest again. On May 6, I thought I heard peeping coming from the nest box. With the noise from all the other birds, it was hard to tell for sure. On May 7 the hen emerged from the nest. I heard the definite sound of young in the box. May 8 found us checking the box and finding two chicks. Both appeared healthy and were well fed. One was larger and probably two days older than the other. Loud peeping came from the nest on May 10, and the parents were both in the outdoor flight. This forced us to check once again, and we discovered the smaller chick was missing. The larger chick's crop was completely empty. This chick was taken and successfully hand raised to maturity.

In 1976, this pair had a terrific breeding season. On March 7, they were sitting, and on April 5 chicks were heard peeping. The box was checked; one chick and one unhatched egg were found. The chick's crop was empty, so he was removed for hand feeding. The egg was left, and the hen went back to nest and sat tight. On April 6 the box was checked; we found that the second chick had hatched. This chick was also taken for hand feeding.

In May the birds went back to nest. It was thought the

eggs were due to hatch on June 17. On June 11 both cock and hen were seen in the outdoor flight. The box was then checked and two babies were found. Their ages were about two and four days old. The parents continued to stay outdoors; for fear that the babies would become chilled, we removed these chicks also for hand feeding. All four chicks were successfully reared to maturity.

This pair had a terrible breeding season in 1977. They had one clutch of eggs in March. In April, the cock and hen were both found in the outdoor flights. The box was checked and two cold eggs were found. The eggs contained fully formed chicks that were dead in the egg. We had a terrible thunderstorm the night before, and this could have scared the hen off the nest. The pair made no attempt at a second clutch.

On March 20, 1978 the greaters were nesting. By March 29, the birds were fidgety and off the nest quite a bit. This we attributed to a disturbance caused by heavy construction work being done about 3,000 yards away. Pile drivers were causing a tremendous amount of noise and vibration. This in turn made us nervous, not to mention the birds, so the eggs were taken and placed under our pigeons. One egg hatched on April 8 and the other on April 10.

The hen laid two more eggs in April. They were also taken and placed under pigeons. They hatched on May 14 and May 17. The chick that hatched on May 17 was deformed and died the following day. The other three chicks were reared to maturity.

PIGEONS AS FOSTER BROODERS

When we had no success in hatching cockatoo eggs in an incubator, it was determined that an alternative method would have to be found.

Because I have had many years of experience raising pigeons and a great amount of success switching eggs and young ones from nest to nest for various reasons, the thought occurred to me that it would be possible to foster the eggs under pigeons. A little research was done, and I read that a cockatoo's body temperature ranges from 105° to 107° Fahrenheit and that a pigeon's body temperature is 107° Fahrenheit. After finding the body temperatures of the two birds to be very close, I next had to consider the egg size.

Choosing the different types of pigeons that we had, the closest in egg size was the homing pigeon. We chose mature pairs that were known to be good sitters, had bred previously and were well acquainted with and established in the loft.

The fact that these brooding pigeons do not recognize or object to a substitution of eggs or young squabs enabled us to transfer them at will. Constant observation was also easily attained. Pigeons, if handled correctly, will tolerate handling of the eggs; additionally, if they are forced off the nest they will promptly return when left alone.

Pigeons will normally incubate their eggs from 17 to 19 days. The cockatoo eggs incubation period is 30 days. After about 15 days, the eggs are switched to a second pair of pigeons which have just started sitting (on their own eggs). This enables us to attain the total 30-day incubation period, with an extra few days for a possible slow hatch.

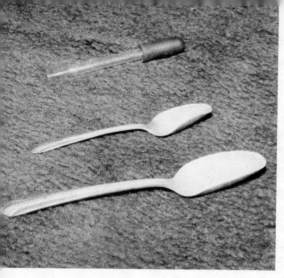

Eye-dropper and crimped spoons—inexpensive necessities in the hand-feeding of baby cockatoos. Below: cockatoo incubator. The rings are used to raise the heat source away from the babies as they grow.

Incubators
and
Feeding
the Young

A week before the eggs are due to hatch, all necessary equipment is set up in our bird nursery. This is a room in our home that is closed off to all traffic and is used mainly for the rearing of our baby birds. Two incubators are set up, and the temperature is regulated to hold a reading of 100.75 °F to 102 °F. This incubator is also equipped with a water pan that provides needed moisture. In one incubator we also include a one-ounce (liquor or shot) glass. It is filled with water and attains the temperature of the incubator. If necessary, this water is applied to the eggs with a Q-tip during the hatching-out process to soften the shell. This is also

used to moisten a chick if it dries out too quickly and sticks to the shell. This preparation a week before hatching allows ample time to make sure that the incubators are functioning and keeping the proper temperature continuously.

HATCHING

When the natural parents appear to be nervous or unsettled and do not appear to be sitting tight, the eggs are removed and placed under pigeons. The fostering pigeons are viewed daily to make sure all is well. From about the twenty-fifth day on, the eggs are inspected closely and quite frequently in search of the first signs of hatching. On or about the twenty-eighth or twenty-ninth day, the first sign of pipping can be found. A chip and pushing upward at the middle of the shell is known as a pip. If at this time you were to hold the egg against your ear, intermittent peeping and tapping noises would be heard.

After the first pip mark has been observed, the egg is taken and put into an incubator. In this way we can observe the chick during the entire hatching process. Whenever removing pipped eggs from the nest for observation or switching, you must position them the same way in which they were found, this usually being the pipped part up. If this is not done, hatching is delayed and death may occur.

HELPING TO HATCH

It usually takes 48 hours for the chick to hatch after the first pip is made. During this time the chick turns and begins pipping with its egg tooth toward the larger end of the egg. After hours of delay, it works its way around inside the shell, pipping as it goes. As it does this it pushes with its shoulder until the eggshell opens and the chick emerges. At this time it uncoils its neck from under its right wing, which is the chick's pipping position.

On occasion a chick is not strong enough to pip and liberate itself from the shell. This is not to say that the chick is weak or deformed; it just may be that the shell is too thick or strong because of varying vitamin and mineral intake on the part of the female parent. Another incident that could occur during the hatching process is that the shell could be pipped but the inner membrane left unbroken or partially broken. The membrane could become stiff or very dry, thus causing the chick in some instances to be unable to hatch out by itself. A lack of proper humidity could also be the cause of a chick's not being able to hatch.

In this case, the pipped chip is lifted off and the skin-like inner membrane is opened a little. This must be done with extreme caution so as not to injure the chick inside. The upper third of the egg (its "fatter" end) is dampened with a Q-tip and warm water above the pip mark; in doing this, you must be careful not to get water into the pip hole.

In one instance, thirty-six hours had elapsed and the chick still had not hatched out on its own. Not knowing the exact time the pip mark was made, we became concerned as to whether or not the chick was trapped or stuck in its shell, possibly from being too dry. After sterilizing our hands and equipment (a small pair of embroidery scissors and a needle) with a strong germicidal detergent, we removed the egg from the incubator and placed it on a paper towel on a table. Using the scissors and the eye end of the needle, we removed the top third of the eggshell, leaving the membrane intact. The membrane was then peeled open, starting around the chick's beak, but slight bleeding occurred and this procedure was stopped instantly. The egg was immediately returned to the incubator. Three hours later the egg was removed and warm water was dabbed all over the remaining shell and exposed membrane. The membrane had become dried out. The chick was placed back into the incubator—and right before our eyes, the chick pulled its head out from under its wing. A few moments later it gave a few shrugs with its shoulders and pushed its feet against the bottom of the shell, pushing its body right out of the egg. It was amazing; the chick performed like a true champion.

You should not attempt to remove the entire body of the chick from the shell. You should only free the head end. This allows the chick time to gain strength, absorb the yolk and free itself from the remainder of the shell.

After the chick has hatched, the temperature in the incubator is lowered. We have found that 96- 97°F is comfortable for a newly hatched chick. High temperatures cause chicks to pant and become restless.

TIME SPENT IN THE INCUBATOR

From the time they are hatched until they are 33 days old, the chicks are kept in a temperature-controlled brooder. The incubators are equipped with two extra spacer rings that attach to the bottom. This adds four more inches to the height, making the incubator into an excellent brooder. With this added height it can be used for a longer period of time, maintaining the desired temperature accurately; this is extremely important.

The chick is kept in a shallow concave bowl lined with a paper towel and pine shavings. The paper towel acts as a cushion around the rim of the bowl, in case the chick should bump his head. It also absorbs a great deal of the wetness from the droppings of the chick. On top of this there is a thin layer of dustless pine shavings; these shavings help to keep the chick dry. A chick in a wet nest will be uncomfortable and will indicate its discomfort by becoming restless and peeping loudly. It can also be seen trying to move to a drier spot. When the nest is clean and dry, the chick will quiet down and go to sleep. This condition would be comparable to that of a baby with a soiled diaper.

The shavings were found to be a good base for dry firm footing, which reduces the chance of "straddle leg" in young chicks. Although many aviculturists trace this condition to a vitamin deficiency, in my opinion it is caused by the lack of proper nesting material. If the chick is left on a fairly smooth flat surface without sufficient nesting material, it cannot keep its feet beneath its body. When kept on a smooth surface, the chick's legs slide out continuously until they are extended at right angles to the body. This causes stiffness of joints and possible bone deformity. The chick loses control of one or both legs and rests mainly on its breast. The use of a concave bowl and nesting material prevents the extension of the legs which causes the condition.

For the first four days of the chick's life, this bowl is kept on the egg tray with the moisture pan below it. This provides moisture which seems to be needed; without it the chick appears to have dry and flaky skin.

The time spent in an incubator brooder varies according to the size of the bird being raised. It was found that a greater sulphur-crested cockatoo chick outgrows the brooder at 17 days of age and an umbrella cockatoo chick at 28 days of age. Once the chick outgrows this incubator, it is put into a larger brooder. This furnishes the desired controlled heat for the first five weeks, at which time the temperature will have been decreased to that of normal room temperature.

It should be noted that as the chick grows the bowl size is increased to accommodate the chick comfortably. The first bowl used is a 4½-inch dessert dish; this is replaced with larger ones until the final 9-inch size is used.

FEEDING THE YOUNG

In order to grow properly, cockatoo chicks must consume large amounts of nutritious food quite frequently. The following formula is a most beneficial one for growing chicks. Other formulas were tried but were found to be lacking in comparison. This formula has been successful not only with cockatoo chicks, but also Amazons and cockatiels as well. The chicks grow at a tremendous rate and are healthy and robust.

FEEDING FORMULA

> 2 cups of high protein Pablum (baby cereal)
>
> 1 cup of high protein dog chow (ground fine in a blender)
>
> 1 cup of yellow corn meal
>
> 1 cup of hulled sunflower seed (ground fine in a blender)
>
> 1 cup of hulled millet seed (ground fine in a blender)
>
> 1 cup of raw wheat germ

Mix all the above ingredients in a covered container and store in the refrigerator. Each day a portion of this mix (¾ of a cup) is put in a small saucepan and is mixed with one cup of water. This is simmered on the stove and stirred occasionally until all the water has been absorbed. Another ¼ cup of water is added and simmered until all of the water has been absorbed. This cooking process should take approximately ten minutes.

Cooking the food, rather than adding warm water, assures you that a chick will digest all the food given. When just warm water is added to the dry mix, the food given tends to dry and cake in the crop, causing impaction. This results from the fact that the liquid tends to be absorbed further by the formula and also is digested first by the chick, forming a dry mass in the crop.

This cooked mixture is then placed into a covered jar and stored in the refrigerator until needed. When feeding a day-old chick, this cooked amount should last two days. The *longest* period of time that this food is used is two days. Anything left over after this time is discarded.

Along with this formula, a high potency multivitamin supplement is given once a day. Vitamins are given only after the chick is four days old. Every feeding of formula also contains two spoonsful of one of the following strained baby foods: garden vegetables, spinach, applesauce or carrots. These are mixed in with the formula as it is being heated for feeding. This provides a balanced and nutritional diet and also aids in digestion and elimination.

MATERIALS USED IN FEEDING

To be prepared for hand feeding, one should have on hand the following:

An electric heat-and-serve baby food dish
Eyedroppers
A demitasse spoon with the sides bent to form a scoop
A teaspoon with the sides bent to form a scoop
A nine-inch bowl
A thin soft cloth.

The electric baby food dish is ideal for heating the formula to just the right temperature (approximately 102°F). When the correct temperature is reached, the dish is unplugged and moved to where the chick is being fed. Once heated, the dish holds the temperature of the food for half an hour. This is terrific when feeding more than one chick, as you do not have to worry about the food's becoming too cold. A chick will not eat food that is cold, and cold food hampers digestion.

The 9-inch bowl is lined with a thin layer of shavings and is used to hold the chick while it is being fed. It is washed after each feeding.

A thin soft cloth is wet with warm water and is used to wash the chick after its feeding. You will notice, when feeding a chick, that it is a bit sloppy. Care should be taken to wash off any formula that sticks to the sides of the chick's beak.

An eyedropper is used to feed the chick for the first two days. I have found that the demitasse spoon works well after this. Some chicks take to the spoon the very first day. When the chick gets larger (approximately 40 days old) a teaspoon is used. I do not use a spoon any larger than a teaspoon, as I have found it to be too messy.

A very young chick's beak is quite soft, and it should be

1

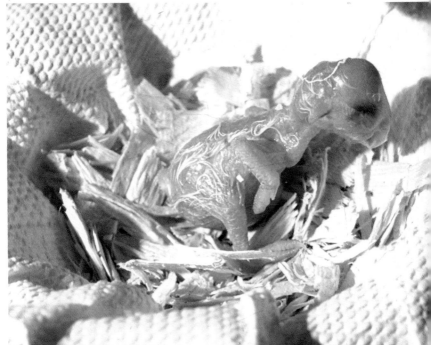

1. A newly hatched greater sulphur-crested chick; wet down covers the chick, and a piece of white membrane from the egg is still on its back. 2. The chick in its nest bowl drying off in the incubator. 3. A 33-day-old umbrella cockatoo chick in its fish tank brooder. 4. umbrella cockatoo chicks in their brooder. Photos by Frank Nothaft.

3

4

treated gently. Feeding haphazardly or with force could cause a deformity of the beak.

The length of time from the time of hatching to the first feeding varies according to the individual chick. Restlessness and frequent loud peeping on the part of the chick indicate that it is hungry. A chick usually becomes hungry approximately six hours after hatching. This starts the feeding schedule of every two hours around the clock for the first 14 days. At this time the chick's crop has grown and the chick is able to consume more food which lasts a longer period of time. The time between feedings is then increased by half-hour intervals as the chick grows. Changes in the feeding schedule can be noted by the eagerness of a chick during feeding and the amount of food left in the chick's crop from its previous feeding. These observations will become second nature to you as you go along.

During feeding a very young chick is weak and anxious. It bobs its head a lot, so you must hold its head. Using your thumb and forefinger, place one finger near each outer ear hole and gently hold the head up while feeding. As the chick grows, it will eat with much gusto. Its wings will be semi-extended and flapping, with a rapid up-and-down jerking of the head as the food is swallowed.

Chicks fed properly grow at a tremendous rate. A brief example of the growth rate of two cockatoo chicks we've raised (a greater sulphur-crested and an umbrella) follows:

	GREATER SULPHUR	UMBRELLA
hatched out	18.20 grams	no weight was logged
10 days old	72.35 grams	56.35 grams
15 days old	143.66 grams	117.25 grams
20 days old	276.67 grams	233.25 grams

Each baby chick should be taken and fed individually in order to give it your full and undivided attention. By doing so, you are sure to handle the chicks properly and avoid the possibility of the chick's falling or being accidentally dropped. A single chick can be observed with more scrutiny in all characteristics of growth. Any abnormalities will surely be noted at once, and appropriate measures can be taken.

A chick should be picked up bodily with one hand and placed in the palm of the other. As the chick gains strength, it will start to grip objects with its feet. When picking up a chick, take note to see whether he is grasping anything with his feet. If so, lift him gently with one hand, opening and freeing his toes with the other simultaneously. Yanking on the chick in order to make him free its grip will only make you succeed in hurting the soft bones in its legs.

THE CROP

The crop on the young chick is transparent. As you feed the chick you can see it enlarge. A chick is fed until the crop is full to within ¼ of an inch below the esophagus. As the chick digests its food the crop becomes smaller and smaller, finally disappearing as it becomes completely empty. Just before the crop is empty, the chick will start moving around and peeping for food. This is the preferred time for feeding, as it is best not to let the crop become empty.

In its baby stage the bird eats so much that the front of its body is pulled down by the weight of the crop. As the bird feathers up, however, the crop becomes less noticeable. For about the first eight weeks, even though the bird has become fully feathered the feathers covering the crop are always parted, leaving it visible. By this time the bird is in its slimming stage; it consumes less food, allowing the crop to contract. This enables the feathers to fill in the nakedness of the crop.

At one time we were forced to bring in and hand-feed a chick that was three days old. The chick had been fed by its

1. 17-day-old greater sulphur-crested chick. 2. The same chick, shown with a 7-week-old albino cockatiel. 3. 23-day-old greater sulphur-crested cockatoo chick. 4. Umbrella cockatoo chicks at around 27 days of age. Photos by Frank Nothaft.

1

2

3

4

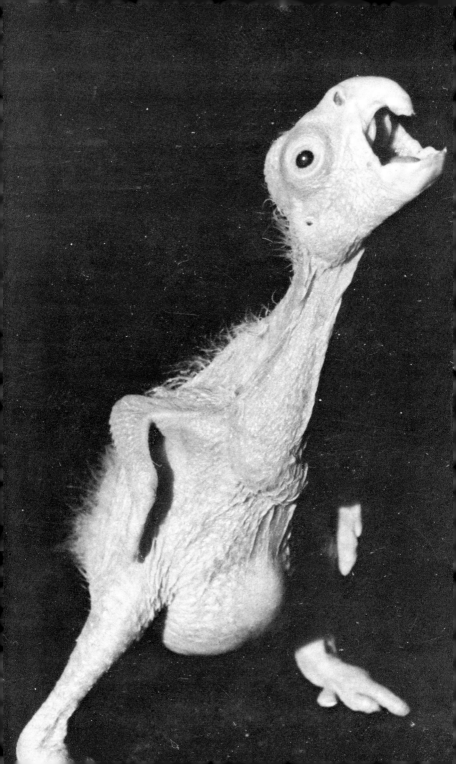

parents and its crop was full. Upon close inspection, it was noted that the crop contained about eight whole hulled sunflower kernels. The chick appeared uncomfortable and seemed to be hungry. A small amount of diluted formula was fed. The crop was massaged, working the seeds in with the formula. This was done because the chick was hungry and the seed in its crop would not digest, causing a blockage known as impacted crop. After this feeding, the chick was passing whole sunflower kernels in its droppings. Every half hour I alternately added to the crop a few drops of warm water and a drop of milk of magnesia, and then honey and warm water and dark molasses. With each administration, the crop was massaged in order to mix these additives in and break up the impaction. This was done for one complete day.

The following day found the chick looking and acting fine, with the crop impaction reduced to half the size. A feeding of formula and applesauce at a very watery consistency was given every two hours. Each feeding also contained a few drops of molasses or milk of magnesia. The crop was massaged during each feeding.

The third day, the first five feedings consisted of warm water and molasses alternated with warm water and milk of magnesia; the crop was massaged. This reduced the impaction to the size of a pea, but whole sunflower kernels could still be seen in the crop. Regular feedings of a watery consistency were resumed for the rest of the day. On the fourth day there was no change in the chick's condition. A thin mixture of formula with a drop of Pepto Bismol and a pinch of fine sifted parakeet grit was fed. All other feedings remained normal. For the next four days the bird digested all formula that was fed. During this time the chick gained almost 32 grams; when it was over, the impaction had vanished.

This greater sulphur-crested chick is thirteen days old and (seemingly, at least) perpetually hungry. Baby cockatoos constantly demand food, and they let you know about it through their piteous cries.

1. Greater sulphur-crested chick at age of 37 days. 2. the same bird, shown with a 2-week-old cockatiel. 3. Greater sulphur-crested cockatoo at 43 days of age. 4. The same bird at 52 days of age. Photos by Frank Nothaft.

3

4

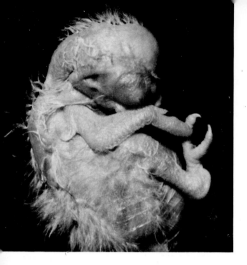

To say that baby cockatoos are unprepossessing in appearance is putting it mildly—but their initial grotesquerie matters little when the birds mature into the handsome specimens like the Major Mitchell cockatoos shown below. Photo at left by Frank Nothaft; photo below by San Diego Zoo.

Growth
of the Young

A healthy baby chick has a bluish tone and sheen to its skin, which indicates good health and blood circulation. If the chick is pale and dry, it is probably weak and anemic. A newly hatched chick is sparsely covered with fluffy yellow down except on the crown of the head. It is very weak and requires a lot of rest, awakening when hungry.

When the chick is ten days old its eyes open a slit, gradually opening more until the eighteenth day, when it can see. The baby at eighteen days old will stay awake longer and will be sitting up on its feet quite sturdily. The

1

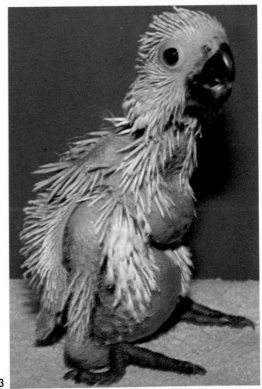

1. A 50-day-old greater sulphur-crested cockatoo that is almost fully feathered; the bird's crest, tail and wings are still short. 2. The same bird with its wings held apart to show that the wing feathers have not fully opened. 3. 32-day-old umbrella cockatoo chick sitting perfectly at ease. 4. 28-day-old umbrella chick being weighed. Photos by Frank Nothaft.

3

4

beak starts getting darker and harder by the nineteenth day. The feet start to become darker at this time.

Pin feathers start to emerge in the wings by the twelfth day. By seventeen days, chest and leg feathers are emerging, and by the twentieth day head and crest feathers can be seen. The chick will raise its crest, which is just stubby pin feathers. At twenty-six days, the wing feathers start to open at the tips. By thirty-two days, the quills are opening all over the body. On the fortieth day, the chick's body is almost fully feathered. It flaps its wings a lot for exercise and raises its crest up and down quite frequently. At forty-seven days, it is picking up pine chips and an occasional seed with its foot and inquisitively nibbling on them with its beak. The baby stands on one leg while sleeping and preens itself on and off most of the day.

SLIMMING PHASE

At about seven weeks of age, the chick arrives at the time when it must slim down in order to be able to fly. Nature provides the chick with the urge to cut down on food and to exercise its wings, which it does with great enthusiasm. The baby is still being fed four times a day, but it consumes very little at each feeding.

At this age, babies should be taken out occasionally and placed on the floor. They love to walk about, exercising their wings and displaying by extending the crest, fanning the tail and cocking the head. This seems to bring them much enjoyment and is an amusing and comical sight to behold.

By eight weeks, the chick is eating small amounts of seed.

USE OF FISH TANKS FOR SEPARATING YOUNG

From the twenty-eighth day onward the chick will have been in the brooder with no heat supplement; it should be comfortable and should do fine at normal room temperatures. The chick at thirty-three days old will become too large for the brooder and should be tranferred to a twenty-gallon fish tank (12½ x 24 x 16″ high). If there is more than one chick, they should be separated at this time. We have found that separating the chicks makes them more dependent and attached to humans rather than to each other, thus making them better pets.

The fish tank is lined with newspaper, and two inches of dustless pine shavings are placed on top. The top of the tank is fitted with a wire cover. A piece of Plexiglas, cut to fit the top, is placed over the wire cover. This Plexiglas cover is used to prevent drafts and can be regulated to adjust the temperature inside. The amount of airflow is adjusted merely by sliding the Plexiglas cover, allowing more or less of an opening on top. The wire beneath prevents the Plexiglas from falling on the chick.

At six weeks of age, still in the tank, the chick is moved from the nursery to the kitchen. This is done so that the chick becomes completely familiar with all household sounds and movements, as this is the busiest room in the house. If the bird is being raised primarily as a house pet, it is best to introduce it to household sounds as early as possible. By doing so, it becomes accustomed to other people and voices rather than to the one person raising it. A bowl of seed is given to the chick at this time. The seed provided is standard parrot mix. Hulled sunflower was tried, but it was found that the chicks showed less interest and took much longer before they were actually eating it. They constantly played with, opened and ate the regular seed much earlier than the hulled.

WEANING

At nine weeks of age, the young bird is placed on a parrot "T" stand. This stand is equipped with an adjustable tray situated below the perch; the tray is designed to catch the seeds and droppings. The tray is raised and set to a fixed position five inches (or just below the bird's tail) below the

1

1. Adult little corella, also called bare-eyed cockatoo, **Cacatua sanguinea.** Photo by San Diego Zoo. 2. 39-day-old umbrella cockatoo with its crest of pin feathers erected. 3. A 34-day-old male and 32-day-old female umbrella cockatoo; the head of the male is larger. Photos by Frank Nothaft.

2

3

perch. This is done so that when the bird falls off the perch it is possible for the bird to learn to climb back up by itself.

Birds this age are very clumsy and uncoordinated, but in a short time they will master the art of climbing. Seed and water are placed in the cups, which are situated on both ends of the perch. This stand is equipped with a cage-type cover that is used whenever the bird is going to be left home alone and during the course of the night.

The youngster is left out on the perch for about eight hours during the day. The rest of the time is spent in the fish tank. After being on a stand for this amount of time, baby cockatoos seem to be tired. A short time after being placed in the tank, they stretch out in their bedding and go to sleep. Within one week, a bird will be adjusted to the stand and the use of the fish tank can be eliminated.

During the time that the youngster is adjusting to the cage and stand, it will be eating seeds well. Baby food is offered twice a day. The bird consumes quite a bit at the morning feeding, eating only a small amount (3 or 4 spoonfuls) at the evening feeding.

By the time the youngster is seventy-five days old, it is usually completely on its own, refusing all offers of baby formula. It looks very much like an adult. On closer examination, it can be noted that clinging to the tip of some of the back feathers is the yellow down of a newly hatched chick. A greater sulphur-crested youngster has one or two gray feathers over the nostrils or on the back.

WING CLIPPING

The bird's wings are clipped at nine weeks of age in order to restrict its flight. This is done before the bird has successfully flown. Usually after four or five times of trying to fly and not being able to go very far, the bird will be content with staying on its perch.

The first eight primary feathers are clipped one inch below the primary covert. This is done on both wings to avoid unbalanced appearance and curved flight, which would be the case if only one wing were clipped.

Since hand-fed young cockatoos are extremely tame, this clipping is done while the bird is sitting on the "T" stand. The wing is held open with one hand and clipped with the other. If your bird will not tolerate this, its body must be restrained (wrapped in a soft, absorbent towel), and the above procedure should be followed.

CLAW CLIPPING

The sharp points of the claws are clipped off for the first time at six weeks of age. After this they are clipped at regular intervals. Ordinary toenail cutters are used, but the specially designed clippers sold in pet shops might be safer. If the claw is clipped back too far, into the quick, bleeding will occur. Should this happen, hydrogen peroxide applied with a Q-tip will usually provide excellent results.

This task can be performed on tame birds while they are on the stand. Otherwise, restraint must be applied.

MISCELLANEOUS REMARKS ABOUT YOUNG COCKATOOS

All babies are lovable, and each individual has a slightly different personality. A youngster will adapt easily to its owner's expectations.

I prefer to take the egg and hatch the youngster out myself. This is done in order to imprint humans on the baby from the first day of its life. When immature, the baby thinks of you as its parent. As the youngster matures, it then thinks of you as its mate, indicating so by displaying and regurgitating when you are near.

All members and guests in our house are encouraged to handle and play with the young birds. This accustoms the youngsters to different people and handling, making them tame to everyone.

A medium-size fiberglass airline dog carrier makes an ex-

1

1. The author and one of her cockatoos enjoying a playing/training session. 2. A young umbrella cockatoo that has its crest and body pin feathers raised because he was frightened. 3. A Leadbeater's cockatoo male displaying his crest. Photos by Frank Nothart.

2

3

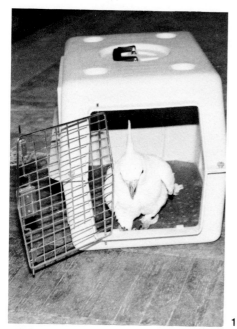

1. A cockatoo in its travel carrier. 2. Confinement of a cockatoo to a cage should not be continuous; the bird should be taken out frequently and provided with attention and affection. 3. One of the author's cockatoos playing dead.

1

2

cellent carrier for a tame cockato. Such carriers can be purchased from pet shops. With this carrier, you may safely take your pet cockatoo with you on your travels.

When housing a tame cockatoo in a cage, it is best to leave the wire grate in place. If the grate is in place, the bird does not step into its own droppings, tear up the paper in the tray, foul its plumage, etc.

For the health and well-being of a pet cockatoo, it is essential to keep the bird company and keep it occupied. We always keep the bird with an ample supply of pieces of branches to chew on. These are tree limbs, about 1 inch thick, cut into 3- or 4-inch lengths. This gives the bird something to do, and it will not become bored easily when kept in the cage. A pet should be taken out of the cage as often as possible for both its enjoyment and yours.

My best results in breeding birds were obtained by reading all material that became available to me. I observed the birds as much as possible and drew my conclusions as to what was ideal for my birds and myself.

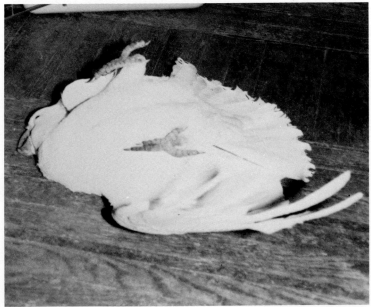

3

Cockatoos in most parts of their range are in danger of decreasing in number, so the breeding of cockatoos by aviculturists can be environmentally valuable as well as satisfying and potentially rewarding. Three relatively rare and hard-to-breed species are shown here: 1. *Calyptorhynchus funereus baudinii,* the white-tailed cockatoo. 2. *Calyptorhynchus magnificus magnificus,* the red-tailed cockatoo. 3. *Probisciger aterrimus goliath,* palm cockatoo. Photos 1, Vogelpark Walsrode; 2, San Diego Zoo; 3, Dr. Herbert R. Axelrod.

SUGGESTED READING

DISEASES OF BUDGERIGARS, (TFH/671), Cessa Feyerabend, ISBN 0-87666-953-4. Comprehensive guide for those who keep parakeets. Topics on recognition of specific diseases and how to treat them. 5½ x 8, 123 pages; 104 color photos, 67 b/w photos, 17 line illustrations.

BUDGERIGAR HANDBOOK, (TFH/H-901), Ernest H. Hart, ISBN 0-87666-414-1. Almost every color variety is shown in full color photographs; showing, breeding, and every other subject of importance for the budgie enthusiast is completely covered. 5½ x 8½, 251 pages; 104 color photos, 67 b/w photos.

TAMING AND TRAINING BUDGERIGARS, (TFH/AP-1880), Cessa Feyerabend and Dr. Mathew M. Vriends, ISBN 0-87666-960-7. For the beginning and experienced bird fanciers who would like to teach their birds to talk and do tricks. 5½ x 8, 192 pages; 54 color photos, 63 b/w photos.

BREEDING BUDGERIGARS, (TFH/PS-761), Cessa Feyerabend and Dr. Matthew M. Vriends, ISBN 0-87666-960-7. A respected classic, completely updated, particularly the chapter on genetics. Many new color photos show the various color varieties resulting from different breeding combinations. 5½ x 8, 192 pages; 81 color photos, many b/w photos.

FEEDING BUDGERIGARS, (TFH/AP-400), Cessa Feyerabend and Dr. Matthew M. Vriends, ISBN 0-87666-971-2. This useful text provides an excellent understanding of budgerigars' nutritional needs. It presents an overview of the digestive process and recommendations about what to feed your bird and what to avoid. 5½ x 8, 128 pages, 39 color photos, many b/w photos.

ENCYCLOPEDIA OF CANARIES, (TFH/H-967), G.T. Dodwell, ISBN 0-87666-952-6. This book is intended for the new canary fancier. It covers breeding systems, heredity, and environment, types of exhibition, birdrooms, and cage fitting. Hard cover, 5½ x 8, 281 pages; 48 color photos, 28 b/w photos.

ENCYCLOPEDIA OF COCKATIELS, (TFH/PS-743), George A. Smith, ISBN 0-87666-958-5. An excellent book designed to help beginners and experienced aviculturists alike. In addition to material on maintenance, feeding, housing, breeding, and disease control and treatment, there is a fine section on genetics and selecting breeders. Hard cover, 5½ x 8, 256 pages; 58 color photos, many b/w photos.

FINCHES AND SOFT-BILLED BIRDS, (TFH/H-908) Henry Bates and Robert Busenbark, ISBN 0-87666-421-4. EVERY important soft-billed cage bird is discussed and illustrated in color. Used throughout the world as an identification guide. Hard cover, 5½ x 8½, 735 pages, 246 color photos, 159 b/w photos.

BREEDING THE COLORFUL LITTLE GRASS PARAKEET, (TFH/KW-006), Ralph V. Smith, ISBN 0-87666-982-8. The first book to deal specifically with this subject, it is the result of several years of first-hand experience by the author. Covers feeding, breeding, identification—everything you need to know. 5½ x 8, 96 pages; 38 color photos, many b/w photos.

HALFMOONS AND DWARF PARROTS, (TFH/PS-647), William Allen, ISBN 0-87666-424-9. For the person who buys his first halfmoon parrot and may be interested in another one. 5½ x 8, 80 pages; 31 color photos, 30 b/w photos.

LORIES & LORIKEETS, (TFH/PS-773), Rosemary Low, ISBN 0-87666-980-1. A comprehensive volume which contains descriptions of all the species and subspecies of this group. Emphasis especially given to the experiences of aviculturists the world over in breeding these birds. Practical, comprehensive, fascinating. 6 x 9¼, 180 pages; 54 color photos; appendix of names in English, French, German, and Dutch.

ENCYCLOPEDIA OF LOVEBIRDS AND OTHER DWARF PARROTS, (TFH/H-1014), Dr. Matthew M. Vriends, ISBN 0-87666-972-0. This book by a noted Dutch ornithologist covers in detail every lovebird species and subspecies. All aspects of keeping and breeding are covered as well as the characteristics, behavior, and interesting historical sidelights about each bird. 5½ x 8, 256 pages; 42 color photos, many b/w photos.

LOVEBIRDS AND RELATED PARROTS, (TFH/H-1015), George A. Smith, ISBN 0-87666-974-7. A scientific but practical treatment. Characteristics, habitat, world distribution, care, behavior, and breeding of each species are included. 9 3/8 x 6 3/4, 192 pages; 30 color plates, 18 line drawings. Also available in a soft-bound edition.

MACAWS, (TFH/KW-003), Loren Spiotta, ISBN 0-87666-975-5. An excellent guidebook about the largest member of the parrot family. Covers every Macaw species and every important aspect of Macaw maintenance, feeding, housing, breeding and disease control. 5½ x 8, 96 pages; heavily illustrated with color and b/w photos.

AFRICAN GREY PARROTS, (TFH/KW-018), Paul R. Paradise, ISBN 0-87666-977-1. Concentrates on what any owner needs to know about maintenance, feeding, training and health care. 5½ x 8, 96 pages; many color and b/w photos.

TRAINING AFRICAN GREY PARROTS, (TFH/KW-025), Risa Teitler, ISBN 0-87666-994-1. Practical, sensible step-by-step approach to teaching this popular parrot how to talk and act. 5½ x 8, 96 pages; many color and b/w photos.

AMAZON PARROTS, (TFH/KWK-012), Paul R. Paradise, ISBN 0-87666-985-2. A new text devoted to the best known of the New World parrots, among the most widely kept of the true parrots. Covers many species. 5½ x 8, 96 pages; 36 color photos, many b/w photos.

PARROTS IN CAPTIVITY, (TFH/H-1018), W.T. Greene, M.d., updated by Dr. Matthew M. Vriends, ISBN 0-87666-979-8. A 1979 reprint of Greene's classic work which appeared in three volumes between 1884-1887. No part of the original text has been eliminated or changed in any way. This edition includes all three original volumes in one book, and an index with additional notes by Dr. Vriends has been aded. 6¼ x 9¾, 544 pages; contains all of the original color plates which appeared in the 1884-7 edition.

PARROTS AND RELATED BIRDS, (TFH/H-912), Henry J. Bates and Robert L. Busenbark, Third Editon edited and expanded by Dr. Matthew M. Vriends, ISBN 0-87666-967-4. This book has more color photographs of parrots than any other book. New editions are issued regularly, with new color photos added to each new edition. This third edition includes updated nomenclature, and has been restructured for easier reading. Hard cover, 5½ x 8½, 494 pages; 160 color photos, 107 b/w photos.

PARROTS OF THE WORLD, (TFH/PS-753), Joseph M. Forshaw, ISBN 0-87666-959-3. This immense book covers every species and subspecies of parrot in the world, including those recently extinct. Almost 500 species and subspecies are illustrated in full color on large color plates. Hard cover, 9½ x 12½, 584 pages; almost 300 large color plates, many line illustrations.

BIRD DISEASES: An Introduction To The Study of Birds in Health and Disease, (TFH/H-964), Drs. L. Arnall and I.F. Keymer, ISBN 0-87666-950-X. A highly specialized book which requires a thorough education in biology to be understood, but experienced bird lovers can recognize symptoms and diseases from the many illustrations. Hard cover, 6 x 9, 528 pages; 99 color photos, 304 b/w photos.